Irish
Proverbs

Little Books of Ireland

I'm not as green
as I'm cabbage looking

If you dig a grave for others
you might fall into it yourself

A man with no wit
has little on a pig

Ther's no bone in the tongue
but it often struck a man down

The truth comes out
when the spirit goes in

He'd step over ten naked women
to get at a pint

The World is a stage
but the play is badly cast

A man that can't laugh at himself
should be given a mirror

You'll never plough a field
by turning it over in your mind

Women begin by resisting
a man's advances
and end up
blocking his retreat

Burning the candle at both ends
will soon leave you without a light

A Nation's greatest enemy
is the small minds
of it's small people

On the ladder of success, there's always someone on the rung above using your head to steady themselves

You can take a man
out of the bog
but you cannot take the bog
out of the man

sh Proverbs

ok and Jacket Design by Brian Murphy

Picture Press.ie Ltd 2016

blished by Real Ireland Design
cture House
17 Bullford Business Park,
coole, County Wicklow.
vw.realireland.ie
o@realireland.ie

CIP catalogue record for this book is available from the
tish Library.

3N 0946887-500

r a wider selection of proverbs we would suggest
ms of Irish Wisdom: Irish Proverbs and Sayings
Padraic O'Farrell
blished by Mercier Press